REVELATIONS

A NON-FICTION SHORT STORY
by

J. P. HAMILTON

Dedication

This book is dedicated to my children, Letisha, Omar and Key, my little surprise. You are the lights of my life, my reason for being. You have all my love now and always!

Special thanks to my mother, Joan, Richard, Alanna, Nkenna and Nate for their love and support throughout this unexpected journey!

It may take some time,
To find your voice,
But once found,
What a beautiful sound.

J. P. Hamilton

Introduction

This short story came to life as the result of a series of daily emails that I wrote to my beloved children, Letisha and Omar when I needed to be away from home. This was only the second time that I was ever away from them because we normally all travel together, thereby eliminating the need to write.

Where I go, they go, except for the time that I won a trip to the Bahamas with a group of Avon representatives. Loving, dutiful mother I may be but who in their right mind would forgo a four day, all expenses paid trip to Nassau, Bahamas sans children or spouse? Not me!

My intent in sending the emails was for us to stay connected and to let them know what was going on and how I was feeling. In the end, it was the best decision that I could have possibly made because it really helped me emotionally. The entire experience of putting my thoughts into words first on paper and then on the computer screen was very cathartic.

Although I didn't realize it at the time, the emails were inadvertent daily journals that gave me an outlet to release my thoughts and my feelings, of which there were many. I've never thought to myself, you know you should write a book. Believe me when I tell you that I'm not always this verbose, though some may disagree. It's true that less is more, but sometimes you get a story out of your verbosity.

Prologue

I was born in Trinidad, a beautiful, sunlit, tropical island in the West Indies. The island is nestled between the Caribbean Sea and the Atlantic Ocean, off the eastern shores of Venezuela. Though small in size it has a number of very unique features. The island is known for its rich reserves of petroleum and natural gas, and of course carnival. There's the La Brea Pitch Lake which is the largest natural deposit of asphalt in the world, one of only three in existence on Earth. It's one of the best places in the world to see Leatherback Turtle hatchlings. It's also the island where calypso and limbo originated and, as stated on an old Jeopardy episode, it is the birthplace of the only acoustic instrument invented in the 20th century. And the answer is: What is steel pan?

Tobago, Trinidad's sister island, has the Nylon Pool which is best described as a natural swimming pool in the middle of the ocean. In 1976, long before Usain Bolt hit the world's stage, the first hundred metre Olympic champion from the Caribbean was Hasely Crawford of Trinidad & Tobago. The first black woman ever to be crowned Miss Universe is Janelle Commissiong from Trinidad & Tobago. These are just some of the things that make Trinidad such a special place. An island paradise that's worth visiting!

I spent my formative years living on the island until the age of eleven, when my two younger brothers and I moved to Canada to live with our mother, who had emigrated four years earlier. With the aid of a maternal aunt who had sponsored her, my mother decided to leave Trinidad to work in Montreal, Canada. She made the move in an effort to secure a better life for herself and her children.

When mom decided to leave us, she entrusted my care to her best friend Cynthia, who is also my godmother. My younger brothers, Richard and Derek, were left in the care of our maternal grandmother, Iris, who literally lived across the street from where I lived, until all three of us eventually immigrated to Canada. At the point in time where this story begins, it had been many years since my last visit to the island of my birth.

1 - The Trip Down

My mother, Joan, arrived at the airport to see me off, dressed well and looking beautiful. I really wasn't expecting her to come all that way with the intent of only saying goodbye; after all there are phones for that purpose. But it's just like mom to do that, to do the unexpected. She said she would have liked to have accompanied me on the trip for moral support and, of course, because she loves me. She wanted to make sure that her first born wasn't alone as I embarked on my fateful trip. But mom had just returned a couple of days ago from spending three weeks in Trinidad herself. She'd gone to visit her twin brothers and while there,

REVELATIONS

she'd heard through the grapevine that Roy wasn't well. She had contacted his wife and told her that she would like to visit him in the hospital. Not surprisingly, his response was, "Why?" and "No!" Not sure in which order. Mom told me that had she known that I was going to travel down to Trinidad so soon, she would have stayed to be with me, but I made a last minute, unexpected decision to go. I didn't necessarily want to go but then I thought I would regret it if I didn't go and see him. I was right!

While we waited for my turn to check in at the Caribbean Airlines counter, a man I didn't know, who was walking by, waved at me and smiled. It seems like such a simple thing that when a man smiles at you, you should just smile back. But alas it's not that simple. In my experience sometimes I have to be careful how I respond.

Do I genuinely smile the wide show of teeth smile or do I just move my lips slightly in the semblance of a smile, like I do for photo IDs. It's the projection and promise of a smile but not a full-on commitment. For me it's not always an easy decision because depending on the returned smile, the recipient can misinterpret your response and take it as an invitation to stop, talk, etc.

J. P. HAMILTON

Sometimes it doesn't even matter whether you return the smile or not because the initiator of the exchange will continue to engage, as though you waved them over with your arms open wide.

On this occasion the man who smiled at me was older and walking away from us and from my years of experience it seemed like a harmless enough smile. I smiled back, to be polite, and the man kept walking away. After he'd passed by, I turned to mom and asked her, "Who is that man who seems to think he knows me?" When I asked the question, I didn't necessarily think that she knew who he was, but she didn't even hesitate for a second. Mom said, "He's your Uncle Auburn."

Really?! You'd think that I would know my own uncle, right? Wrong. You see, I've never met him before, even though we've all not only been living in Canada for decades, and we all live in the Greater Toronto Area, probably less than an hour apart. Coincidentally as it turns out, an aunt and that same uncle were also on the flight to Trinidad with me that night. Before taking off from Toronto, I learned that another paternal aunt died of kidney cancer three years ago. This was just the

REVELATIONS

beginning of the pearls of information that I would glean during this memorable trip back home.

As luck would have it, and I'm not referring to lady luck, I was recovering from an ear infection, the only one I've ever had to my knowledge. I believe my ear got infected while I was in downtown Toronto on a lunch hour shopping break. It had been an extremely windy day that created a funnel effect as I walked between the tall buildings. I don't have scientific evidence to back up this conclusion, but I deduced that it was the only thing that made sense.

Let me tell you that flying in an airplane, while recovering from an ear infection is absolutely, unequivocally not advisable. Unfortunately for me, I always suffer from ear pain while flying but I'd never experienced anything as bad as that before. Even with the use of ear plugs and chewing gum like my life depended on it, I was in excruciating pain. I would prefer to be knocked out for a flight than go through that again!

I wonder if that's a possibility. It's definitely something to think about for another time if I have an ear infection and I absolutely, positively had to fly somewhere. You just never know what could happen. I could win a trip to Fiji or Tahiti or some exotic place and happen to have an ear infection at the time, but you know I am taking that trip!

My ears hurt so much that I wished that I had someone there with me to hold my hand and offer me some modicum amount of comfort. Even though it wouldn't have lessened the pain it would have helped to make me feel better to at least have someone to commiserate with.

I arrived at 10:30 a.m. but the plane had arrived earlier than scheduled so I ended up having to wait for my ride. I didn't have international cell phone coverage and I wanted to make sure that I wouldn't be waiting too long. I looked around to see if there was anyone who could perhaps help me.

I approached a local gentleman who was standing close by leaning against a wall waiting. I smiled at him and asked if he had a cell phone that I could possibly use. Unexpectedly, he generously proffered two cell phones for me to choose from, a BlackBerry and an iPhone. I was pleasantly surprised and since I know absolutely nothing about the workings of the former, I gladly accepted the iPhone and made two quick calls. After

REVELATIONS

finishing my calls, I returned the phone to the kind stranger, smiled again and thanked him for his generosity. Then I found a seat where I could sit and wait. Auntie Cynthia, with whom I would be staying, was on her way to pick me up. Thank you Jesus!

Sitting there all alone at the airport waiting for my ride, somehow it felt like I was always alone. There I was with all those strangers walking by and milling about, waiting for friends and loved ones, but there was nobody there waiting for me. No wait a minute; they're not all strangers after all.

Some of those people were actually family members with faces that are somehow familiar and others that should be familiar but that I've never seen before. I should know them, and they should know me, but they don't nor do they really seem to care...ditto. After all wasn't I a stranger to the man who links us all? He didn't care to know me nor even give a damn, so why on earth should they?

It's strange that all these people are part of my family, and there were so many of them too, including the aunt and uncle who'd arrived on the flight with me. There were at least eight of them at the airport and it appears they were still waiting for more family to arrive, but none of them were waiting for me though. At one point Aunt Gloria, at whose house I've slept many years ago, literally pointed me out to someone else. My aunt glanced at me and indicated in my direction with her head, no hello, no nothing.

In the end they're just like everyone else, perfect strangers, well maybe not so perfect. After the funeral they'll all return to that place once again, the land of strangers who don't interest me in the least, any more than I interest them. I am once again on an island virtually alone, even more so now that the link between us is gone.

Coincidentally, while I sit here composing this email, a voice over the radio has just reported that Patrick Swayze died of pancreatic cancer. The radio announcer stated that it is the most virulent form of cancer with a survival rate of five years and five percent. I'm not a betting person, like some people I know, but those aren't very good odds. It just so happens that my father succumbed to that same form of cancer also. Small world!

REVELATIONS

Anyway, I just wanted to say I'm alive and well and the tropical weather here does amazing things to the hair and skin. I can see it already and I've only been here all of eight hours. I think it's the moisture in the air that just makes your skin and hair more radiant and glowing and I am loving it!

I hope the two of you are behaving yourselves, watching out for each other and staying safe. I wouldn't want anything to happen to either one of you.

2 - Out & About

Auntie Cynthia took me to visit my father's widow today; it was my first time meeting her. The house was very interesting and unexpected. It was the fourth house up a fairly steep winding road and the three houses that we passed on the way were mere shells, no indication of their former glory, assuming there was ever any glory associated with them to begin with.

There was an iron gate supported by two concrete walls outside their house and both walls were covered in Bible scriptures in large print. The house behind the wall was old and clearly in need of a complete HGTV makeover. There didn't appear to be any life therein, besides the

REVELATIONS

vicious dogs that raced to the gate to see which of us they could bite first. Through the metal gate we could also see a cat and two kittens in the yard. We later found out that there used to be twelve dogs in total, but the pack had been whittled down to the current six. Lucky us!

The barking dogs had heralded our arrival and a woman came out of the house, settled the dogs down and ushered us in through the gate. Since I'd never previously met or spoken to my stepmother before, after we left the house, I had to ask auntie, "What's her name?" Euralene welcomed us into her home and stated, almost immediately, "She looks like Roy. She has his eyes." I do? It wasn't stated but I believe I also inherited the family nose. And that's all that I'm going to say on that topic!

Euralene didn't appear to be that old but she looked tired and still obviously struggling with the unexpected loss of her longtime companion. To my surprise, she mentioned that my father knew what day my birthday fell on. She said that he would say, "Jemma is thirty-five years old today." Or I guess whatever my age happened to be that particular year. I don't know if he said the same thing every year, and I didn't ask, but it's a small comfort knowing that he at least thought of me once a year. I've never received a birthday card, birthday wishes or anything at all from him, except for the eyes of course. Imagine me rolling those eyes.

We sat listening to her as she spoke about his last days, that he had needed blood, and having to purchase said blood. According to my stepmother, in Trinidad you must replace any blood that the hospital gives you at a ratio of 1:1. If that's the case I think the Trinidad Blood Services motto should be, "It's in you to give, and ya better bring some back."

During the conversation Euralene listed off the names of his family members like a verbal family tree, and I was, once again, struck by the fact that I knew nothing of him or any of them. It always makes me feel like I'm the forgotten one or the ignored one and I wonder why things turned out that way. It's at those times that I feel sad and I have to fight back tears.

I have always wanted to get to know my father and have a chance to talk to him because I really know absolutely nothing about him, other than the odd tiny snippet of information that I gleaned from mom over the years. Auntie and I left shortly afterwards and made plans to

REVELATIONS

return another day, to talk some more and look at pictures, since I've never seen any and have none.

As we left the house and walked through the gate, I could no longer hold them back and I let the tears fall silently down my cheek. It's a good thing that I always carry a small pack of tissues in my purse, no matter what size my purse is, depending on the season. If not auntie or mom are always prepared to supply one, if the need arises and I can't get to mine quickly enough. It's strange that I've cried more in the past few days than I can remember crying my entire life.

The next stop on our itinerary was to the hospital to visit an ailing maternal uncle. On the way there we stopped at Kentucky Fried Chicken because I needed a cold drink since the heat and humidity was really testing my Caribbeaness (is that even a word?). I would say that I'm borderline failing the test, but I think I still have a chance to pull up my grade.

As usual I was astounded by the Trinidad menu prices. A two-piece meal is $23, and Omar's favorite popcorn chicken meal costs a whopping $32. Although it would be six dollars and change with the Canadian conversion, it's still shocking every time to see those numbers on the menu board. What's even more shocking are restaurant menu prices and price tags at the grocery store.

On a previous trip five of us had dined at Ruby Tuesday, of all places to go eat on a Caribbean island, and the bill came to over $1800 TT (Trinidad & Tobago dollars). I remember taking a picture of the eighteen blue hundred-dollar bills that I'd fanned out on the table. It wasn't my money, but it just seemed like a lot of money and it's not like it's a fine dining restaurant or experience.

There is a little bit of comfort though after calculating the conversion to determine what the actual cost would be in Canadian dollars. On average the exchange rate that you'd receive at the bank or at a foreign exchange counter is 5:1 for the Canadian dollar and 6:1 for an American dollar. Although during this trip I found out that there are certain locally known stores that offer even higher rates but only for the almighty American dollar.

Intuition is a valuable tool to be heeded at the best of times but often we ignore our intuition and forge ahead, which can sometimes be detrimental to our health. Many years ago mom's brother, Uncle Winston, didn't feel like going to work one day. As he tells it an inner voice told

REVELATIONS

him to stay home but in the end, he got up, got dressed and went to work anyway. His job was in construction and that day, while on the job site, a wall fell on him and he was left permanently paralyzed from the waist down. That's a pretty tough lesson to learn!

I've known for a long time that mom and Richard know things and can sense things before they happen and even as they're happening. Sometimes they seem to interpret the information from dreams but at other times it appears as though they just pluck the information out of midair, like from a text bubble that was floating by. For instance, during my first pregnancy somehow Richard knew when I went into labour. I wish he would just hurry up and share the winning lottery numbers already.

I have to admit that I'm not as attuned and dialed in to my intuition as they are, but they've been practicing for a very long time. Most of the time I don't even remember the dreams that I've dreamt, though we purportedly dream every night. I have had the odd dream that seemed utterly ridiculous at the time but that did eventually come to fruition.

J. P. HAMILTON

I woke up one morning and I remember having a dream in which I was taking care of a baby girl. I could see her pretty little face as I was holding her in my arms and in the dream, it felt like she was my child. I was confused and I thought the dream was ludicrous because my baby days were over. Been there, done that and I have the stretch marks to prove it. I thought maybe it was my daughter's baby that I was caring for and picturing in my head. Alas that dream came true and I've been loving and caring for my little girl almost three years now.

One night I dreamt that a friend came to me as I was lying in bed; he bent down, held my hand and kissed me on the cheek. That morning I woke up remembering the dream vividly and somehow it felt like he was saying goodbye. Later that day I found out that he'd died that morning. There were still words to be exchanged between us, things still left unsaid. One of the last texts that he sent me read, "You are a great mother." It was a sudden, unexpected compliment that made me feel really good and warmed my heart. I'm so glad that he thought of me and came to say goodbye on his way to the sweet hereafter.

REVELATIONS

Uncle Winston had been recently hospitalized because he was suffering, along with his other ailments, from cysts in the area of his kidneys. You could see by the frequent grimaces on his face that he was in a lot of pain. He told us that he was still trying to decide if he should have an operation in an attempt to stop the pain. His doctor advised him that the cysts were very close to his spine and because of the proximity it would be a risky surgery. Although, if you're already paralyzed, as he is, what exactly is the risk? If I'd become a doctor maybe I'd know the answer to that question. Perhaps the risk is that there could potentially be more paralysis above the waist if there was further damage done to his spine?

Uncle Winston had no way of knowing that I would be there, in Trinidad, never mind visiting him in hospital but he recognized me right away. He said that he'd told mom that I would come to see my father. He also said that he recognized me because as he put it, "You have the same face since you came into the world." I guess that's a good thing? As I looked at him lying in the bed, for the first time I could see some similarities to mom that I'd never noticed before. In particular, they have the same type of teeth which are shorter and narrower than mine.

J. P. HAMILTON

I know that sounds strange but it's true nonetheless. I have never really thought about mom's teeth or paid any real attention to them. I mean I know she has teeth; I've seen them enough times but that was the extent of my attention and interest. My teeth are definitely not like my mother's, so it made me wonder if I inherited my teeth from my father. The answer to that query came the following day when Aunt Glenda said to me, "You have the same nice teeth like Roy." Yay, more similarities! The universe had responded to my unspoken question. If I had to get something from him at least I got the good stuff, there's worse stuff I could have inherited. I'm counting my blessings!

3 - Things That Make You Go Hmm

I sit back and marvel at the driving and the drivers on this island. Talk about wild and crazy but definitely interesting and competent. The drivers are as good as it gets and there's always someone, driver or pedestrian, ready and willing to offer advice and direction when necessary. There are a lot of cars squeezing by in tight spaces and what appears to be a lot of really close calls. Oftentimes it can best be described as organized chaos, at least in the smaller side streets. There are instances where a one-way street has been converted into a two-way street, but someone either forgot to remove the 'No Entry' sign or they just couldn't be bothered.

Nevertheless, somehow everyone knows what they are doing, and they arrive at their destination safely. Basically, drivers and pedestrians do whatever they feel like doing a lot of the time.

I've often thought that it would be really cool to drive a fast car on a racetrack and push the pedal to the metal. I love speed and have been known to push it on the highway. I consider myself to be a good driver and I'm very comfortable behind the wheel of a car, van or even a small school bus but I wouldn't want to drive here. I would find the experience too stressful and I'm quite comfortable being driven around enabling me to sightsee while I'm here.

My sister, Alanna, sometimes makes fun of me when we're driving somewhere, and I take the curve of the ramp to the highway at a higher speed than would necessarily be advisable. She always ends up slanted in her seat, but I know she exaggerates sometimes to prove her point. She says, "Your kids don't even move from their seat when you turn a corner because they're so used to your driving since they were little." Maybe, but they were also trained from childhood to immediately put their seatbelt on as soon as they get into anyone's car.

REVELATIONS

It's probably true that I do drive fast but it's obviously a family trait because neither she nor Richard knows what it means to drive slowly either. We all drive fast, and the blame can be laid directly at mom's doorstep because she definitely isn't any better. She was a speed demon with a lead foot when she used to drive, way back when Jesus was a boy. I'm just kidding mom.

Auntie mentioned that she'd hired a car to come and take us to the beach one day. Sometimes she schedules trips ahead of time with her usual driver to take her directly to her destination, depending on how far she's going. This saves a lot of the time and energy that it takes switching taxis for each leg of the trip.

If we go, the destination would be Maracas Beach, which is a very beautiful beach, more than an hour's drive up in the mountains. The idea that you need to drive high up into the mountains, to go to the beach just boggles my mind. How does the water stay up there, doesn't it all have to flow down eventually? Logically, it just doesn't make sense to me.

As is the case with some of the beaches, the water at Maracus Beach has very strong currents so it can be dangerous if you're not careful. If we go, I'll be one of the careful ones since swimming isn't one of my strengths. In other words, I can't swim. Well I did take swimming lessons years ago when we were going to take a Caribbean cruise, and at the end of the course I could successfully swim from one side of the pool to the other. Somehow though, I couldn't tread water to save my life and that's a big problem since the whole purpose of swimming is to save your life. I guess that's a bit of a failure.

There's also a chance that we might visit Tobago, the beautiful, tourist attracting, sister island of Trinidad. I'm really looking forward to going there. I did visit Tobago once twenty-five years ago for my 'honeymoon'. Your father and I fell for each other during one of my early trips back to the island and we had been corresponding for a while. The marriage was a spur of the moment elopement during a subsequent summer trip to Trinidad and no one even knew we were married for over a year. Eventually the cat was let out of the bag because there are some things that you just can't hide, like the impending arrival of a baby! Yeah...that actually happened!

Auntie, my godmother, is an admired, well respected woman and a pillar of her community. The phones in her house ring constantly, all day long, from sunup to beyond sunset, since it's pitch black by 6:00 p.m. here. In the early afternoon the phone rang and this time the call was for me.

The caller was Aunt Gloria, the aunt who flew down on the same plane with me, the head pointer at the airport. After identifying herself she gave the phone to her sister Glenda who said that she doesn't know me, but she would like to stop by to see me later in the day. I was surprised to get the call because Aunt Gloria certainly had time to come over and speak with me at the airport, if she'd chosen to do so. I said sure they could stop by for a visit.

It had been a very long day and I was tired, so I laid down on my bed and fell asleep around 8:00 p.m. while watching television. No one had shown up for the 'viewing' and the phone rang after 9:00 p.m. I bet you can guess who was on the phone. My aunt apologized for not coming by and she commenced to ask how many children Richard I have respectively, for the eulogy. Seriously?! The funeral was less than twenty-four hours away! She also went on to talk to me, the niece she's never met, a virtual stranger, about her children, her daughters, her son, the doctor in England and then she said we would see each other tomorrow. I don't think she actually expressed condolences about the passing of my father, but I guess we all know that there was no closeness or real loss; since there'd been nothing there almost from the time I exited my mother's womb.

This is now the second day in a row that two different aunts have mentioned that there are two doctors in the family. When I was asked what my daughter was studying, I said, "She wants to be a teacher or a lawyer." The response was, "Well, we need a lawyer in the family. " Well thank you very much for the input. Letisha, you now know what you have to do. Law school here she comes!

As it turns out the doctor in Trinidad is actually a phlebotomist, and as far as I'm aware that's the technician who takes your blood at a medical lab. Perhaps to practice phlebotomy here you first need to secure a medical degree. Who knows? I certainly don't. Once upon a time I wanted to become a doctor. From childhood as far back as I can remember it had always been my dream. I was going to be a doctor and drive a silver Jaguar; the two ideas were indelibly intertwined in my young mind.

REVELATIONS

I had applied, was accepted to and attended the University of Toronto where I obtained my Bachelor of Science degree in Biochemistry & Microbiology. The dream had still been alive and well but the student loan debt from just four years of university was too daunting for me to consider proceeding further, so the dream died a fairly quick death. Should I have mentioned that? Glory hallelujah, perhaps now there's an author in the family. Yippee! That would be great but it's really such nonsense isn't it?

4 - The Morning Of

I woke up around 6:30 a.m. after having fallen asleep early the night before. It was already light out and it's very hard to sleep late with all the noise outside. Auntie's house sits at the apex of a hill, right at the corner where two streets cross and created a busy junction. It's a single-story home with four bedrooms and one bath. Once upon a time auntie had even constructed a small school in the backyard. After a number of years of operation, the school had eventually closed.

A lot of the houses, most of them anyway, have rows of bricks with cut-outs in them to let in the breeze. Sorry but I don't know the correct architectural terminology for said bricks. The closest analogy that I can think of is

REVELATIONS

when children create snowflakes by folding paper and then cutting pieces out of the paper. When completed the paper is unfolded and the result is see through patterns on the page. Well it's exactly like that but instead of paper it's cement bricks with shapes in the middle of them. Sure, this allows the breeze to flow through and helps keep the house cool but unfortunately it allows various flying insects, including mosquitos, to come and go as they darn well please.

All the windows of the house are open so you can hear each and every sound from outside. It's just a cacophony of sound. There's the loud, and I do mean loud, music booming from the cars with their motors revving as they zoom up and down the street, some at speeds you don't hear outside of NASCAR. There's the barking coming from all the neighbourhood dogs of which there seems to be a surplus.

On top of that it literally sounds like every rooster in Trinidad is crowing their morning hello to the world. The never-ending hammering in the nearby house under construction, and the ringing of two separate phone lines in the house just adds to the constant reminder of humanity alive and living. I'm sure there are some other sounds mixed in that I've missed describing but I think you get the idea.

I'm very fortunate to be able to stay in my own private space, in the only childhood home that I remember living in with Auntie Cynthia, ostensibly my adopted mother, as she was to me for those years. My brother and I lived with her for a total of four years after mom left to seek a better life in Canada. To have her take me under her wing, once again, to shepherd, guide and watch over me during this very emotional time in my life is really appreciated. I've never told her, some words just don't need to be said, but she must surely know that she holds a very special place in my heart and mind, forever and for always, in this lifetime and in any to come.

Since I was up so early, and I was looking for something to do to kill time, I perused the endless stacks of VHS movies on shelves across one wall of the bedroom in which I slept. I finally settled on a copy of the movie *Regarding Henry* and I decided to watch it. It's an interesting, dramatic and thought provoking movie that, coincidentally, I've been meaning to watch again having first seen it many years ago.

REVELATIONS

There were so many movies to choose from and I just had to pick that one. At the end of the movie I realized that it was probably not the best choice to watch at that time. The movie ends when the father, played by Indiana Jones himself, Harrison Ford, decides that he needs to spend as much time as he has left with his neglected daughter, whose first eleven years he basically missed due to his work.

In a few hours I'll be viewing the body of my father who missed out on forty-five years of my life without a second thought. It was just another reminder, like I needed one, and reason for me to feel sad. I'm sure this afternoon will not be easy for me. As much as I would like to think that I'm not affected or that I don't care, it has become obvious to me that I am affected, and I do care. The sea of relatives that I'm about to be immersed in will be interesting, if nothing else.

5 - The Funeral

Doreen, who is a friend of mom and auntie, picked us up in her car and drove us to the church. She would also drive us to and from the cemetery, to and from the house where the reception was to be held and back to auntie's house at the end of the day. I sat in the front seat with Doreen at the wheel, where auntie always insists that I sit. Even when we take taxis, which is every time we leave the house, I move to sit in the back out of respect for her. If the front seat is available, she always goes to the back and I sit in front because as she puts it, I need more leg room since I'm fairly tall at 5 feet, 9 inches.

REVELATIONS

My father's widow, Euralene, and Doreen are also good friends due to the fact that they are all members of the same congregation. Their church is my father's church and it is, therefore, hosting his funeral. Coincidentally it happens to be the church that I grew up attending with auntie as a child, a couple of times each week and twice on Sunday. The church where I was baptized, where I had my first crush and where I won sword drill contests as a child.

A sword drill contest was held each Sunday during the morning service. Everyone who wanted to participate in the contest would be directed to hold their closed Bible up in the air. The minister would announce a chapter and verse and the participants would flip through their Bible to find the page as quickly as possible. The person who found it first would stand up and read the verse out loud. For every correct verse found the reader would receive one point. The weekly totals are tallied and at the end of the contest, which runs for months, a winner was announced.

I was very adept at finding the passages quickly due in part to my previous memorization of the books of the Bible for recitation during a morning service. Guess who won? I was the overall winner and I fittingly received a beautiful engraved Bible as my prize. I still own the Bible and cherish it as much as I did when I first laid eyes on it. As such, the church is very familiar to me, and of course with "a face that hasn't changed since I was born," there are always people who recognize me when I attend there.

While driving to the church Doreen was speaking to auntie and she nonchalantly told her that while they were having a conversation Euralene told her, "Ya know, he love her ya know." I, of course, innocently asked, "He loved who?" As an answer to my question Doreen kept her right hand on the wheel and extended her left index finger in my direction. I was stunned. If it were possible for me in my black skin to turn pale, I surely would have done so.

In some distant part of my mind I thought that was it nice to hear that my father loved me, maybe it even meant something, but it was without a doubt the most God-awful time to hear it. As we arrived at the gate in front of the church a white hearse pulled up directly in front of our car. We had arrived at our church together, my father and I, for the first and final time.

REVELATIONS

It was a wet and rainy day, the day they buried my father. It was a wet and rainy day, the day they buried my father. I kept repeating those words to myself like a mantra, in order to remember them later when I could write it all down to compose this message to you. As we waited in front of the church for the pallbearers to take the casket out it hit me again that this would be the last time that I would see him. To save my life I couldn't have identified when the penultimate time was.

I was just fine last night as I composed my thoughts and put pen to paper. The television was on and there wasn't a tear in sight, but as I sit typing this latest message to you the tears started flowing again. I guess the wound is so fresh and the memory is still right there, just below the surface.

The one and only funeral that I attended was also here, in my childhood, prior to our move to Canada. I had no preconceived ideas as to how I would feel, or what I would be thinking. I thought I would be emotionless, separate and detached because I assumed, erroneously, that I felt and would feel nothing. I mean living apart from a parent, with whom you have had no contact, for over forty years should mean that there are no emotions. Right? Wrong…totally wrong! Obviously, I don't know myself at all because the tears started flowing, and the emotions started swirling before I even entered the church, and they didn't let up until close to the end of the two-hour long service.

I tried to ready myself as I walked up to the casket and prepared to look in; I had to look inside because I had come a long way to not at least look at him. I've seen him so infrequently in the past that I'm not sure that I could have distinguished him out of a crowd of men. Seeing his wrinkled, lifeless face in the casket awoke no discernible sign of recognition in me. There really aren't any words to adequately express how it felt seeing my father like that, for the first time after not having seen him for so many years, just lying there, dead in that coffin. It was heartbreaking!

That was the singular, most emotionally devastating day of my life thus far. The one thing that could possibly surpass it would be if it was a family member therein, someone who I was indeed close to, someone who I grew up with and truly loved. That's how difficult it was. I don't think I was crying for him as much as I was crying for myself, for what I had lost and what I never really had. Crying for what could have been but wasn't and what now could never be. Crying for what everyone else who spoke of him seemed to have experienced from him but that I never had.

Other than his name I know pretty much nothing about him. Not his height, his favourite food, his shoe size or even his date of birth. Did he have a favorite colour or song? Did he like to read? Who knows? I did eventually ask mom when his birthday was, and she told me that he was born at the beginning of October just like she was. With the additional information that I've since gathered I can say that's fundamentally where the similarity between the two of them begins and ends. While she is calm, gentle, generous and even tempered, he is unpredictable, rash, miserly and volatile.

As Roy is being eulogized, he is described as a lively, vivacious, helpful, caring, family man who was always there for you and who was always willing to lend a helping hand. To me they were describing a complete stranger. I thought, what about me? Why not me, what did I do to deserve the absolute opposite of all that? Was I not worthy of your caring or love at all? Wasn't I your flesh and blood, your firstborn? Didn't I deserve that most basic human attention too? All I have ever experienced of him is the total opposite of all of his alleged attributes.

Even the minister, who led the service stated, "Roy was like a father to me, always there to help and support me. When I had a bad accident and my car was totaled, he was the first person to offer me financial assistance." Seriously?! How many times over the years could I have used a helping hand or even a miniscule amount of support? Seeing that Roy was like a father to him, I guess that makes us siblings. What a joke!

Auntie, who sat next to me, passed me tissues and tried to comfort me and one aunt or the other who was sitting close by would touch my hand or my shoulder, but I was inconsolable. Usually I am, if nothing else, the epitome of decorum with a calm demeanour but in that place and time I was emotionally devastated. The sounds of all those words of praise and gratitude just kept crashing against my eardrums.

As more utterances of admiration continued to pour out of their mouths, the resulting thoughts that swirled through my head just kept the tears flowing and flowing. I've never cried that much before in my life and I hope to never do so again. It's emotionally exhausting and overwhelming to be so affected amongst a group of actual strangers regardless of any genetic affiliations.

REVELATIONS

I learned that Roy was a very religious man, a devout Christian, so much so that he commissioned the writing of the scripture verses on the perimeter walls of his home. He was also described as entrepreneurial, a bit of a daredevil and a family man, well obviously, not to all his family. Mom had mentioned in the past that he rode a motorcycle and that he was very proficient at it, having won numerous trophies. This is one of the only things that I knew about my father. Until a couple of years ago I didn't even know what day his birthday fell on.

For my entire life, my greatest wish has been to have my father's love. I've seen so many examples of positive father daughter relationships on screen, and I've longed to be adored, cherished and supported in that way. I remember as teenagers Richard and I took our first trip back to Trinidad for a visit. We were exhausted from the long plane ride. Anyone who has experienced the rigours of international travel knows that it's an extremely long, tiring day.

At that time my father was a transit bus driver, and he literally, and I do mean literally, took us from the airport to every bus terminal that he worked out of, to parade us around and introduce us as his children to his coworkers and friends. In my mind's eye I can see us still wearing the same clothes in the pictures that were taken to mark the occasion at the airport. You would have thought that he was proud of us but his lack of attention before that day and for the rest of our lives totally negated that idea.

Years later, after I'd given birth to my first child, his first grandchild, I wrote him a letter in an effort to start a dialogue and to perhaps, at last, create a bond between us. I wanted to let him know he was a grandfather and I had hoped that it would be a bridge, a beginning to who knows what. I wrote that letter to which I never received any response.

There wasn't even an acknowledgment that he received the letter. Not even a note that said, "Yeah I got your letter. So you had a baby…big deal." There was nothing, not ever! Years later I did ask him if he'd received the letter and his response was, "Yes. I chose not to respond." That was the end of the subject because I didn't say another word about it.

From those few words softly spoken by Doreen in the car, on the way to the funeral, it seems, perhaps, that I had his love all along and I just never knew it until now.

REVELATIONS

If you can call any of that love. It would have been oh so nice to have heard words of love come from him, just once, and not as hearsay. Perhaps he just didn't know how to love, or perhaps due to perceived differences he had with my mother after their divorce, he chose not to show it. Maybe in his mind he thought that mom had packed our heads full of all kinds of negative things about him, as divorced parents sometimes do with their child(ren) to turn them against the other parent.

The fact is mom has never talked about her time with my father at all unless I've asked her a question and I've rarely broached the subject. The experiences she had as his wife were too full of neglect, mental trauma, hunger and attempted violence against her person as was recently disclosed in conversations. I've always wanted to sit down with him and ask a whole slew of questions that have held space in my mind in the intervening years. I have some more insights now and a couple more answers than when I arrived here two days ago, but some of those answers just went with him to the grave. Bye daddy!

6 - The Day After

Today was a day of rest and relaxation with not too much going on. A respite after the events of the past few days, yesterday in particular. I basically spent the day lazing about the house in my bed reading, relaxing, watching movies and just trying not to think too much about anything. The computer in auntie's bedroom hasn't been working for a while and she finally got a computer repair guy to come in and fix it. I'm certain that if I wasn't staying with her, she would have kept putting off fixing it, like she had already been doing for a long time.

As usual auntie cooked us a delicious meal for our culinary pleasure. Today it was fresh stewed chicken, sautéed pigeon peas with white rice and a beautiful

REVELATIONS

salad made with watercress, cucumber and tomatoes. She went to the market this morning and bought some more provisions including the fresh chicken to cook. For the most part meat and fish are purchased fresh for meals and not frozen for later use. And they don't eat leftovers for days on end like we do at our house, but I think sometimes the food actually tastes even better the following day.

A practice that I never see except when I'm visiting auntie is when she removes all the seeds from the cucumber while preparing salads. I've never asked her why she does it but I'm guessing that it's a precaution against diverticulitis. It's a condition that occurs when small pouches that formed in the lining of the digestive tract becomes infected or inflamed and can affect older adults more frequently. Ingesting seeds can exacerbate the issue so that may be the rationale for her practice.

Mom suffers from a bad case of diverticulitis, so much so that one day she was experiencing severe stomach pains and she was rushed to the hospital by ambulance. She'd undergone an emergency surgery procedure and after the operation the surgeon told her that the diverticula, the pouches that form in the lining of the colon, had burst and the pain she was experiencing was due to sepsis.

He said that without the immediate surgery that was performed on her she would have died. I'm glad she was decisive, took action and received the medical attention that saved her life. This is an ongoing medical issue for her, so she has to take any and all precautions necessary to maintain her optimal health and to prevent a reoccurrence.

I am constantly looking around at the people and cars going by while I'm sitting on top of the gallery wall of auntie's house. What's called a gallery here is called a porch in Canada. The covered gallery is enclosed by a short wall that's roughly the height of a balcony rail and it's made of concrete. It's just wide enough to sit on with your butt hanging off on either side a bit, depending of course on the size of your butt. Since childhood I've always liked sitting up there with my legs across the top of the wall to people watch.

It's a pretty busy corner so there's always traffic and people going about their daily business. There's a building across the street with a residence upstairs and a shop underneath that sells groceries and other sundries.

REVELATIONS

The store is quite busy with shoppers coming and going all day long. Also, people stand right beside the concrete wall surrounding auntie's house to wait for taxis passing by and they almost always acknowledge you with a smile, a nod of the head or a wave of the hand.

As the scenery passes by while we're driving or walking down the street, I just marvel at the fact that I'm actually here, in Trinidad again. I've been wanting to come here for so many years, eighteen years in fact but who's counting. There was this feeling that I had, and I kept telling everyone that I'd be taking a trip down this year. I didn't know how, I didn't know when and I didn't know why but somewhere deep inside, I just knew that I'd be coming back this year. What has always stopped me from making the trip hasn't been a lack of motivation or disinterest but for financial reasons. There are very rarely any cheap flights from Canada to Trinidad and the cost for the three of us to travel just wasn't in my budget.

I always intended that you would accompany me, since the last and only time you were here you were only five and not quite two years old. Tisha, you may have a vague memory of your grandfather and Omar, of course you were too young at the time, so you have none. It's too bad that you couldn't have taken the trip with me, but it would have broken you both up to see me as upset as I was yesterday, and I wouldn't want you to see me that way. It's a shame that this is the reason that I finally made the trip after all that time.

There will be a family reunion here next February and Auntie Cynthia has invited us. Little does she know that her family has already planned a huge surprise 75th birthday party to be held in her honour in Queens, New York just after her birthday, in two weeks' time. God's willing we'll be able to attend the birthday celebration and surprise her, and perhaps that will alleviate the need for our attendance at the reunion because a lot of her family will be in attendance at the party. Who knows, perhaps we'll attend both events. Time will tell, as it always does.

7 - Going Down South

Today we're off to San Fernando which is in the southern part of the island and a good distance from where auntie lives in San Juan. Trinidad is shaped sort of like a boot and San Fernando is on the west coast at the front of the boot exactly where your ankle would be. To get there we'll have to travel to Port of Spain, the capital of Trinidad, or 'town' as Trinis refer to it, and from town we'll take a water taxi south to San Fernando. Since both San Fernando and Port of Spain are on the west coast of the island it's a much quicker trip to take to the waterway.

There's a lot less traffic on the water than on the roads, not to mention the pedestrians and traffic lights that slows progress considerably. The water taxis are sleek, modern catamarans that are fast, comfortable and air-conditioned. They sit high atop the water, sturdy and strong but they're graceful as they seem to glide across the water on their way to the station. It is comparable to a comfortable ride in a commuter train cabin; just add water and the accompanying beautiful island views.

After getting out of the taxi we were walking on the sidewalk towards the Croissee and a woman driving her car, stopped the car and addressed me. She said, "Did you buy ya shoes here?" She meant did I buy them in Trinidad. I said, "No." The woman seemed very disappointed with my answer. Then auntie quipped, "You can borrow them ya know." I had no idea that auntie was a comedienne, it was quite funny. I don't know whose shoes she was volunteering to loan out, but it couldn't be mine. I don't lend out my shoes.

The act of stopping a car to speak to someone walking like that would have never happened back in Toronto. I've had someone pay me a compliment while standing next to me at the sidewalk waiting for the light to change. I've even heard footsteps coming behind me to express admiration, but to stop a car and make conversation, that's never happened to me before. Well,

REVELATIONS

if I'm being honest, it has happened before, but it's never been a woman at the wheel, and it wasn't to inquire about my shoes.

I think I was looking pretty cute, if I should say so myself, as I was wearing one of my many homemade outfits. I wore a tribal print dress with a slit halfway down the middle front of the dress. I had paired it with the matching skirt and on my feet, I wore white multi-strapped sandals. They're a gladiator type heeled sandals with gold embellishments that I'd purchased on a rare trip to a mall back home in Etobicoke. The sandals cost me all of $7.50 and it was money well spent indeed, to elicit such an action.

Unfortunately, we went downtown for the 11:00 a.m. water taxi but, as it turns out, the schedule had been changed to a 10:35 a.m. departure. That was the last taxi of the day and we weren't the only people who hadn't received the updated water taxi schedule bulletin. There were a few other potential riders there who looked equally as disappointed as we were. We ended up having to take the bus which is a longer ride, and as luck would have it, we were stuck taking an older model but that didn't have any air-conditioning.

J. P. HAMILTON

We could have taken one with air-conditioning but that would have entailed waiting another half hour. Since neither one of us wanted to wait any longer we got on the bus and found seats where we could sit together. Lady luck must have taken the day off because the rain started falling right after we left the bus terminal, and the steady downpour meant that we had to close the windows which obviously didn't help me with the heat at all. I could feel my Caribbeaness mark slipping again, just a little.

We arrived in San Fernando under intermittent rain and took shelter under the awning of a fabric store entrance. This is a common practice here when shoppers or pedestrians find themselves caught in the rain, and they choose not to walk through it, even if they have an umbrella. As we stood there watching the rain and the traffic go by, a man who belongs in the mad house happened by. Translation: crazy person, sorry I mean a person with mental issues walked by. He stopped on his walk to God knows where and proceeded to kick at a child who was standing close by with his mother, also sheltering from the rain. He then proceeded to curse at the startled mother and child, for no apparent reason. His chant was, "Ya coolie mother cunt." He kept saying

REVELATIONS

it very loudly and repeatedly over and over and over again.

Auntie whispered to me, "It's like he practiced it, and now he's rehearsing it." Her inner comedienne skills showed up once again. Eventually the mother and child walked away but that didn't stop the rant, and after more than five minutes of the performance auntie couldn't take it anymore and we also left the temporary shelter to find another. It's surprising that my religious, former teacher, former principal, seventy-four years young godmother was able to listen to the diatribe as long as she did.

You really had to feel for the innocent duo being so verbally assaulted in that manner, for no apparent reason other than being in the wrong place at the wrong time. I don't know what that phrase ever did to mom but for some reason she hates it with a passion.

After the rain had subsided, we went off to find a taxi, not the marine kind this time, to take us to Gulf City Mall, our final destination and the reason we left the house in the first place. We found one that already had an older woman sitting in the front seat, so we got into the back and, shortly thereafter, a gentleman joined our group to fill all the seats of the car and get us started on our way. The drivers only normally depart after all seats are taken to maximize their earning potential.

If you're in a hurry and you want to leave sooner or because you want more elbow room, you can volunteer to pay for the empty seat. The fare from San Juan to Port of Spain was only $2.00 and the price goes up depending on the distance you're travelling. Alternately you can travel by maxi taxi which is a privately-owned minibus used for public transportation. Maxis cost a little less than taxis and they are always equipped with a booming stereo system and great tunes to liven up your route.

In Port of Spain during the afternoon rush hour the taxis fill up one after the other almost instantly as workers, who don't choose to take the bus, hustle to get home to their loved ones. Taxis are all privately owned vehicles that their owners use for passenger pick up or for scheduled private excursions. It's sort of like Uber without the app, driver information, company control or the associated tracking mechanism.

As the taxi bobbed and weaved through a myriad of hilly streets I began to wonder if we'd happened upon one of those bandits that you hear or

REVELATIONS

read about sometimes. After a while, I noticed auntie looking around at the scenery also and I could almost see her mind working, entertaining the same possibility. Eventually the driver drove up what appeared to be nothing more than a track, backed the car up and dropped the old woman off. Then we were on our way again and we disembarked at the main entrance of the mall. We were both relieved to have arrived safe and sound, neither one of us having alerted the other to their misgivings, though we couldn't have done so in the confines of the car.

The malls in Trinidad are in some ways the same as any other mall, but in other ways they're very different. It's the same as other malls because there are tons of stores in which to shop for everything you could possibly want to buy. It was a really nice experience for someone like me who loves to shop. Let me qualify that by saying that I love a bargain, the bigger the bargain the better because I appreciate quality at the best possible price.

One of the best parts of the mall experience had to be the variety of foods available in the food court; it's like nothing I have ever seen before. This is what's really different from other malls, in my eyes. Yes, there are the regular well-known kiosks represented like KFC, Pizza

Pizza, Subway and other Caribbean booths that you'd expect like Royal Castle. But it was the other kiosks that held the most appeal for me with their plethora of delicious foods on display.

A single kiosk offers macaroni pie, stew peas, steamed vegetables, stewed chicken, fried chicken, barbequed chicken, jerk chicken, pork and beef dishes too. As well as lasagna, callaloo, potato salad, coleslaw, green salads and a variety of drinks. You choose the items you want, the container is weighed, you pay for your purchase and away you go to enjoy your delicious food!

The stores have beautiful clothes and the most gorgeous shoes. The style of clothing and shoes are quite different from what you see back home, which makes it all the more appealing. Did I mention the fabric stores with the most beautiful fabrics to choose from?

When she was a teenager my sister, Alanna, found an old skirt pattern while cleaning her room. The pattern was from a past Home Economics class and, for some unknown reason, she decided to give it to me. Believe it or not that's how my passion for sewing began. I took the pattern, eventually bought some material at Fabricland, followed the directions and I made the skirt.

REVELATIONS

From that point on, I just kept buying more patterns and more material and sewing everything over the years. I was a regular customer at Fabricland and since there's always sales at their stores I was a loyal customer. I used to shop for fabric the way some people shop for shoes. There weren't enough hours in the day to sew all the pieces of fabric that I bought and sometimes I ended up giving material to mom to donate to her friends.

Over the years I've created a lot of clothes including women's suits, dresses, skirts, tops, kids' clothes and even Halloween costumes. The first coat I ever made was a nice warm, lined, fleece coat for mom. There was a time when I practically lived at my sewing machine which is why I used to experience a lot of neck pain from being bent over the machine all day.

My love of sewing goes way back, and the material sold in the fabric stores here are utterly gorgeous to my eyes. They're so different from what I'm used to seeing in the stores back home. The fabrics seem extra special because of their difference and uniqueness compared to the fare available at my usual fabric haunts. Of course, I had to buy material to make curtains when I return home to beautify the house.

J. P. HAMILTON

I was under the impression that I had organically taken up sewing from that first pattern and a natural, God given talent. In a way I'm right because I must have inherited some of that talent from mom, judging from the beautiful dress that she made me, that I'm wearing in the singular baby photo that exists of me.

For the drive back to Port of Spain we caught a taxi that didn't take the scenic route that time and we were promptly dropped off at the water taxi station. While we were waiting for the water taxi to arrive, auntie confirmed my suspicions that she too had been concerned about where the first taxi driver had been taking us. Although she's lived in Trinidad her entire life, she isn't familiar with the San Fernando area, and since I left the island as a child I was definitely of no use with that dilemma.

The water taxi that pulled up to the station was painted in Trinidad's national colours of red, white and black. The air-conditioned interior of the cabin contained high back seats that were well proportioned with ample leg room and made for a very comfortable ride back to Port of Spain. It was a much smoother, quicker trip back to town but even in the rain the earlier bus ride did provide a much richer experience on the roads, where you could see more of the countryside and the infrastructure. The bus also allowed us to see the inhabitants of the island going about their daily lives full of colour and vitality. I experienced the best of both worlds travelling by land and by water because each one had its own benefits and charm.

Well, all's well that ends well. Even though the day wasn't the brightest, and there were a couple of minor bumps in the road, it was an enjoyable day in the end, all things considered. While at the mall I also purchased two ankle bracelets and, taking into account the length of time that I've been trying to find just one anklet, I'd say the trip paid off handsomely.

I've come to the realization that it is a privilege that I'm able to stay in my childhood home. I get to spend this time with my dear godmother, getting to know her better as an adult and catch up on the intervening years. Right now, she's seventy-four years old and as each year goes by there's less and less time to have opportunities to spend in her company. Her thoughtfulness and generosity towards me is deeply appreciated and not taken for granted. I'm blessed to have her continued presence in my life and I'm so happy that you, my darling children, have also had the chance to get to know her when she's visited Canada and stayed with us in our home.

8 - The Matriarchs

Today was designated as the day to visit the older relatives, who all happen to be female. The first visit was to see Aunt Evelyn, who is our eighty-seven-year-old cousin. Next, there was Aunt Remis, a great aunt, who I've met only a couple of times in my life, and she's a young ninety-five. And last, but certainly not least, there was Aunt Edna, another great aunt, who is eighty-nine years old. No matter how far back I search in my memory I have no recollections of any older generation males at all. It's really one of life's great mysteries that somehow all the men died, so very long ago, but the women have remained steadfast and strong anchoring their families.

J. P. HAMILTON

We took two connecting taxies to get to Aunt Evelyn's house in Barataria. She received us warmly into her home even though we weren't expected. You don't necessarily call ahead to announce your arrival, often folks will just show up at your door unexpectedly. Although this could lead to disappointment it's not that big a deal if you're just visiting someone locally. The weather here is beautiful pretty much every day and there's always a nice breeze. Trinidadians or Trinis, as we refer to ourselves, are very friendly, we are quite accommodating and life's good.

The fan in Aunt Evelyn's living room was hard at work blowing from side to side circulating the air inside the house and helping to keep the room cool. We visited with her for a while catching up and talking about family as usual. She talks to mom, her niece, fairly regularly by telephone but she still asked how she was and inquired about her health. The two of them have always had a close relationship and in the past Aunt Evelyn made room for grandma to come and live with her when she had no place else to go. Living so far away in Canada this was a huge relief for mom knowing that her mother had a roof over her head, was living close to family and had a safe place to call home.

REVELATIONS

There's an interesting contrast between these three great ladies on our family tree. I know Aunt Evelyn because I've stayed at her house several times in the past when you were both little. In fact, whenever I visit Trinidad with mom, that's where we normally stay, except for the odd time that we stayed with Auntie Cynthia. If you want quiet and restful then staying at Aunt Evelyn is the place to be. In contrast auntie's house is a beehive of activity a lot of the time and her neighbourhood is a lot busier. There isn't always room available to stay with auntie since she has a lot of family who live abroad, who come to stay with her because she still resides in the family home where they all grew up.

Aunt Evelyn has a good size property with two houses on it. The house in front is divided into two with one side tenant occupied while the other side is kept vacant for visiting family members. The main house which is located at the back of the property has had various renovations over the years. The most recent upgrades extended the main residence even farther back in order to accommodate another living space including a kitchen, bedroom and bathroom.

Aunt Remis' current abode isn't too far from Auntie Evelyn's home, so we were able to take a leisurely walk to her home. She lives in a large, two story house that sits on a corner lot and is jokingly referred to as 'the mansion'. The entire ground floor is divided into rented tenant apartments. The upper floor is the family residence and, as is pretty common on the island, it is accessed by a long, steep stairway at the side of the house. The residence has four bedrooms, kitchen, bathrooms, etc. for when her children come to visit her from the United States.

The upper floor also has a large balcony that was built for her exclusive comfort and use. On said balcony there are several comfy chairs, a television on a stand, a shelving unit displaying family pictures with a stereo system and other personal items. Oh and did I mention the queen size bed? Yes, she has a bed on the balcony where she can lie down and relax anytime she wants to or go to sleep if she so chooses. That is so cool. Who wouldn't want to sleep out on their balcony if they could? Fresh air, a nice breeze and TV too. Heaven!

Even at the ripe old age of ninety-five she is still looking very cute, her toenails are polished, her nails long and manicured, and she has the presence and poise of a queen in her palace. As you can imagine, at her age, she can be a tad forgetful at times. Several times she asked

REVELATIONS

me, "Who are you?" Regardless, she did say more than once that she wants to live to see her hundredth birthday.

She appears to be healthy enough and there's no apparent reason why she won't make it to that age and beyond. After all, her sister, Aunt Colly lived past the age of ninety-eight. I just sat there and kept staring at her, admiring her energy, feistiness and her ability to verbally spar with her assistant while completing her daily crossword puzzles with excellent penmanship.

Our last visit of the day was to see Aunt Edna who it turns out is Aunt Remis' sister and Aunt Evelyn is their niece. The lessons just keep on coming. Aunt Edna has four sons, the two youngest being close in age as is the same with her two eldest sons. The real contrast between these three ladies lies with Aunt Edna who stated that she always thinks about me and looks at my wedding picture, which I guess I gave to her at some point. I've always loved her, and she loves me, so I guess that's the reason right there. I have absolutely no memory of giving her any pictures.

For whatever reason there are a lot of things that I've blocked out of my memory. My mom and my brother,

J. P. HAMILTON

Richard can recall and relate episodes in their lives dating back to when they were as young as two and three years old. I on the other hand can't remember anything. There are a few things that I remember and some events or moments that were significant but for the most part for me it's all a blank. Unfortunately, there are some memories that will never leave me no matter how many years have passed in the interim.

The human mind is a very interesting place; at least I think my mind is. I couldn't have conjured up my father's face to save my life and I saw him a lot in the first few years of my life since we did live in the same house. On the other hand, I can recite with total recall the books of the Bible that I learnt as a child in Trinidad, from the beginning of the Old Testament to the end of the New Testament. And number memorization is another of my unique 'talents'. In fact, there are so many numbers that have accumulated in my head now it would probably take me a couple of hours to write them all down.

One day at a reception job I was going out of my mind with boredom and I kept trying to think what I could do to pass the time. I thought to myself that I should start memorizing Pi because it is an infinite number therefore

REVELATIONS

I'll have material as long as I need it. So I started memorizing Pi for fun and more importantly to keep from falling asleep on the job. As the days passed, I kept adding more numbers until I finally stopped the memorization at 200 digits. Now I can recite them off the top of my head very quickly, but I couldn't tell you the name of my best friend in junior high. Of course, I'm assuming that I had a best friend in junior high.

Years ago, Richard started making a joke by saying, "Jemma couldn't remember yesterday." I've reminded him of that line quite often when it suits me, which is fairly frequently. The truth is he's right, sometimes I just wipe the slate of my mind clean like the event never took place and I have to be reminded of things that occurred. Lucky for me my brother's and my daughter's memory banks are like computers that never run out of space; they keep all our shared memories and remind me of them when necessary.

One of Aunt Edna's younger son's name is Walter and he has always been one of our favorite cousins. Whenever we've visited Trinidad, we could always depend on him to take us here, there, and everywhere we wanted or needed to go. He was like our own private tour guide on the island. There's no question or ambiguity about it, Walter would be there to be our guide, protector and bodyguard if the need arose. There was a special bond between myself and Walter and I think it's my connection to him that keeps me close to Aunt Edna's heart.

The bond was forged years before during another trip to the island. At that time, I'd needed a safe place to stay because of the threat of a man with a knife, who sat all day in front of the house where we were staying. It was a very bizarre event that happened for reasons unbeknownst to me. Unfortunately, the man with the knife was my father.

To this day, I still have no idea why he did that, nor do I understand the rationale behind his behaviour. Perhaps he had mental health issues, I have no idea, and the incident has never been brought up or discussed. I don't know enough about him to proffer a diagnosis but there is ample evidence to support that interpretation.

Sadly, Walter and his brother Leroy were both killed years ago, separately and violently. Walter was being constantly harassed and bullied by a man who worked at a prison. One day I guess Walter had had enough and he got into a fight with the guy. According to mom, the

REVELATIONS

knower of all things, Walter was winning the fight and the man took out a knife and stabbed him in the heart and Walter died.

Leroy, Walter's brother, wasn't tall but he was dark and handsome. Think of Tupac or a young Treach, of Naughty by Nature, and you get the picture. Fairly close to the anniversary of Walter's death Leroy was robbed by a friend who also shot and killed him. The friend was caught, incarcerated and subsequently died in prison.

I've always regretted that at the time I couldn't attend Walter's funeral. As you can imagine Aunt Edna became apprehensive and safety conscious after the violence that was visited on her two younger sons. She rents the top floor of a house, where she lives with and takes care of Walter's three children and her great grandchild. Right now, she's dealing with a serious termite infestation on top of everything else that she has on her plate.

At the age of eighty-nine, when she should be relaxing and enjoying her retirement, she is the owner of no property and she's still dealing with diapers and misbehaving children. Her two granddaughters have attitude written all over their faces, and she told us that at times they take off for days on end without her knowledge or consent, before finally returning home. Personally, I think her grandson is the worst because he often screams at the top of his lungs seemingly without justification. As though that isn't enough, he also throws and destroys her things, including furniture, just for the hell of it. He looks to be about three years old. Can you imagine dealing with that crap at eighty-nine years of age?

9 – A Walk Down Memory Lane

There are so many recollections here in one of my childhood homes. I have an album full of pictures of the years spent with auntie. It's very nostalgic sitting in the living room watching television, in the same space that holds so many memories. There's the piano and bench that I'd sat on many times as I practiced, to the best of my ability, the lessons that my piano teacher had taught me.

There's the dining room table where we ate all of our family meals together. Every Sunday morning, like clockwork, we attended the morning church service then we would return home around 2:00 p.m. to consume the delicious dishes that had been prepared earlier that morning. In contrast to the North American practice the big meal of the day takes place in the early afternoon and not at dinner time.

The dining room table was the centerpiece of remembered birthday parties that were held when I was a little girl living with auntie. My birthday falls a couple of days after one of her nieces, who is about the same age as I am, so auntie would hold joint birthday parties for us every year. On those occasions I wore one of my pretty dresses just like when we attended church services on Sunday.

In addition to the clothes that were purchased for us in Trinidad, mom also made sure to send us beautiful clothes that she bought in Canada and shipped to us. The neighbourhood kids who attended the same school with us were all invited to the parties. There was always lots of food, drinks, games to play and presents to open. Of course, there was also the obligatory birthday cake with candles for us to blow out.

Sometimes things you don't remember doing are forever immortalized in print, a permanent visual testament of past activities and adventures. Browsing through the

REVELATIONS

various photo albums in the living room cabinet was a trip down memory lane, at least a trip from the age of seven or so because there aren't any of me before that age. The only picture that I am aware of from my infancy is a black and white photo of a baby girl, her hair braided and adorned with ribbons, wearing a pretty, frilly dress sitting behind a row of flowers.

Recently I spoke to mom about the photo and I asked her why there aren't any others. She said that in those days there weren't a lot of cameras and when photos were taken, they were taken to give away. She also said that the photo was taken when I was sixteen months old, that she made the lime green dress that I'm wearing, and she arranged to have it taken at a studio. If it weren't for this photo there would be none at all. It took me many years to track one down and I had a copy printed for my photo collection.

I'm only aware of three people who had a copy, my cousin Judy, Aunt Iris and Auntie Cynthia. I'm very grateful to have such a cute baby picture that also displays my mother's love and care of me at an early age. I'm sure there are many people who have no photos at all, so I feel blessed!

10 - Curtain Call

As if she hadn't already done enough, this morning auntie surprised me by producing two tickets, for us to attend an evening performance at Queen's Hall Performing Arts Theatre in Port of Spain. To my joy and surprise she was taking me to see an exhibition of flamenco dancing.

I've never attended a professional dance show before, so I was really looking forward to the prospect of the night's entertainment. We both got dressed up for the evening's event and looked our best as we left the house. Auntie had arranged for her usual driver to pick us up and transport us to the hall.

REVELATIONS

It was another lovely, moonlit night. The driver took a circuitous route that traversed the hillside allowing us to see Port of Spain from a different vantage point, in a whole new light. Is there anything more beautiful than seeing a cityscape below from the overlooking hills at night? Somehow everything looks beautiful and magical at night with all the lights lit up in the buildings, on the bridges and in the reflective glow of the streetlights.

Auntie had no way of knowing that along with rap, calypso, steel pan and jazz I have a particular fondness for Latin music. One of the most enjoyable periods of my life was the two years that I took ballroom and Latin dance classes. The classes were only once a week, but I was so happy during those classes that I was always giggling like a schoolgirl experiencing her first crush. I had the privilege of participating in a couple of Pro-Am (Professional/Amateur) competitions with my instructor accompanying me as my partner; those weekends were truly magical.

I bought material and patterns and I made myself two dresses for the competition. The Latin dress was a short, sexy, spaghetti strap number and for the ballroom dances I made a long, full skirted dress; both were made from different sparkly burgundy material. I've always been a fan of the music and the accompanying dances and I've always wanted to learn. When the opportunity presented itself, I was ecstatic. It was so much fun and such great exercise at the same time that I went from wearing size 14 to size 10. Losing weight was never more fun!

Having previously taken Latin and ballroom dance classes, auntie's gift of a night of flamenco was a wonderful experience for me to behold. It couldn't have been more appropriate if I'd made the choice myself because it's exactly what I would have chosen. It was a beautiful hall, we had good seats and I sat there almost pinching myself, unable to believe just how lucky I was.

The colours of the beautiful clothing worn by the dancers, the rhythm and the precision of their movements was hypnotic. They seemed to use every tendon and muscle in their bodies from the tips of their fingers to the soles of their feet to interpret the music. Their arms, legs and body moved in time with the music creating an alluring almost poetic motion. The sure staccato sound of the dancers' shoes tapping against the floor was mesmerizing. With my eyes glued to the stage I could've stayed there all night. It was a veritable feast for our auditory and visual senses, a truly magnificent

REVELATIONS

evening, and the absolute perfect way to end a not so perfect trip.

11 - Saying Goodbye

Leaving Trinidad was really bittersweet but it was time to go home. I'm quite happy to be going back home to Canada, to sleep in my own bed, to see my beloved children, my mother and the rest of my family who I love and who all love me unconditionally. I'm going to miss being here on this beautiful island where there's so many places that I've still never visited.

When you get here there are so many people to see and visit with and somehow you never do all the touristy things. I still need to visit the rainforest, the bird sanctuary and return to Tobago to visit the Nylon Pool for a start. I really want to go back to Tobago because the last time I visited with the ladies (Judy, Ann, Doreen and mom) we bought ice cream at a grocery store that was just the most scrumptious ice cream I've ever tasted in my life. It's been quite a few years, but I will never forget it. The flavor was pumpkin coconut and I do not eat pumpkin pie but oh my God it was so delicious!!!!! I don't have the words to tell you how amazing that ice cream tasted. I'll say this, if it were possible for me to fly to Tobago and pick up a case and bring it back home; I'd do it in an instant. I absolutely have to experience it again. If the manufacturer of that ice cream is reading this story, feel free to get in touch!

It really turned out to be a good trip, considering the reason that I went in the first place was to bury my father. It had been eighteen years since I was last there and I hope my next visit will not take as long or be as emotional.

I really enjoyed getting to spend time with my godmother, Auntie Cynthia; she was like a second mother to me. She has bestowed upon me more love and affection than any of my paternal, blood relatives. I've always been under the impression, erroneously, as it turns out, that I lived with her for four years. I now understand that I started living with her before mom immigrated to Canada, beginning around the age of six, so I lived with her for five years.

J. P. HAMILTON

It was quite a shock that I've never known this before. I also always thought that both Richard and I were sent to live with her when mom left Trinidad. If I hadn't taken this trip I would probably never have known because it sure hadn't come up in any conversation in thirty-five years.

When I was about four years old my cousin Michael used to pick me up from home and we would walk to my school which was miles away from home. Auntie and mom had been longtime friends and she was a teacher at my school. Since the school was located not far from her home, she suggested to mom that I could go and live with her. They agreed that I would stay with her during the week to attend school and go back home on the weekends.

When mom decided to emigrate it just made sense that since I was already living there, I would continue to do so. My maternal grandmother, Iris, was living in a small place, which was coincidentally in a building about 50 feet across the street from auntie's house. Mom left my younger brothers, Richard and Derek, to live with our grandmother. I was really surprised when auntie told me that after I had been living with her for some time, I asked her if Richard could come and live with us and that's how we both ended up living with her.

As we drove up the winding roads into the mountain towards Maracas Beach auntie pointed out the sights along the way. It was a pleasant drive dotted with houses on the hillside, some seen and some only hinted at by driveways disappearing between the trees. Houses of all sizes, from small to grandiose, were sitting on the mountainside often in precarious positions that didn't seem safe but still offered shelter to their occupants.

At one point on the upward journey auntie pointed across to a distant mountain and declared that I'd accompanied her on a twelve-mile hike there, when I was four years old. She said something to the effect that I was a real trooper, walking along and sometimes being carried, when I grew tired, by one of the older children on the trip. I was under the misconception that I'd never hiked in my life before, but it turns out I have. It's probably going to be the last time because hiking is not my cup of tea…nor is tea for that matter.

Auntie was such a big part of my life for so many years, more years than I even realized, and we sort of lost touch when we moved to Canada. During one of our many discussions she said that I'd spoken to her about my relationship with her nephew, and that she and his mother had been planning a wedding for us. This was another surprising discovery because I don't recall telling her about us and I had no idea that the marriage was sanctioned. I told her that it was for the best that a lot of money hadn't been spent for a wedding, since the marriage was doomed almost from the beginning, for several reasons.

The day before leaving Trinidad auntie and I visited Euralene once more. We went back primarily to look at photos of my father. While we were there, I asked my stepmother if my father wasn't interested in me, and she said, "He did love you, but he just didn't know how to show it." I wonder if he was any better at showing love to her.

While I've spent my life thinking and believing that he wasn't interested in me, he may have been thinking the same thing in reverse. It's strange how things happen in life sometimes, I've always had a hang up about my father and his disinterest in me. I've always wanted a father to love me, to be there for me and although I don't know him and never have, I love him too. Sometimes life happens and you may or may not have any control over it, but I won't spend the rest of my life living with regrets.

While we were visiting my stepmother, she said that Roy didn't want to spend money for this or that medically related cost, and that he didn't have the money to spend. I believe that any money he had he kept to himself, and indications are he had a lot. She had no way of knowing that he did have money which is not only selfish but quite deceitful. Also judging from the house and manner in which they lived, it doesn't give the impression of any means whatsoever.

From all outward appearances he hadn't spent a red cent to make any improvements to the house that they called home for over thirty years. Apparently, money was spent for the creation of the scriptures on the wall in front the house and nothing else. Of course he had a lot of money to loan and help others who he judged to be worthy of his largess.

There have been two father figures in my life, one biological and one of the step variety. In the normal mathematical world where I live, quite comfortably I might add, one plus one should equal two, but in this case one plus one doesn't even equal one tenth. For a little girl with a need and a desire to reach out and embrace that illusion called father, an illusion that has always been somehow just out of reach, it has been a cold reality.

I have no idea if my father had a will, if he included me in his will or even if he had anything to will to anyone. I have been told that he was a 'lender' of money and, according to auntie he's offered her thousands of dollars to borrow over the years. It appears that not only were they good friends but that he was a bit obsessed with her, to the point that at times she had to keep him at a distance. That being said, they talked often about various subjects including investments that he'd made and, in turn advised her to make in real estate. Perhaps no one really knows what he did or didn't have or did or didn't own. The information may have gone with him to the grave.

At this point it doesn't even matter, although, I have to admit that it would be nice if he did leave me something. It would be useful and would in some small measure help alleviate the ambivalent feelings that I have around the issue of my father. Lord knows that it would be wonderful to know that he wanted and

REVELATIONS

planned to do for me in death, what he didn't do for me in life.

Things move slowly in Trinidad and if there is something to inherit, then I have to believe that I'll get it. Either way, I am very glad that I travelled down to attend his funeral which was a sacrifice yet to be paid for. I thank him for my name and for the only thing that he's ever done for me, helping to give me life. I know that the blend of his genes combined with mom's genes helped make me the fabulous person that I am. I'll never regret going back home to see him one last time. Love you daddy!

12 - The Aftermath

That fateful trip for my father's funeral was more meaningful than I could have ever imagined, it was also the last time that I saw those three great ladies alive as well. I'm so glad that I took time during that trip to go and visit with them to see how they were doing and hear about what was happening in their lives. Aunt Edna lived to see her ninety-third birthday, Aunt Evelyn her eighty-ninth and Aunt Remis her ninety-eighth.

Euralene and I have kept in touch since that first meeting. The day of our last visit to to her home she'd asked me for my contact information, and I'd shared it with her without any expectations. I was truly surprised when I received the first phone call from her. She is a kind, gentle, thoughtful, God abiding woman who has never had any children of her own and who has welcomed me into her life with genuine warmth and kindness. She has actually shown me more attention and consideration that I've ever received from Roy. Then again, any miniscule amount of attention is more than he has ever shown.

We talk on the telephone a few times during the year usually around birthdays, Mother's Day and Christmas. Whenever I go to Trinidad, I always visit her at her home and I usually sit with her at the morning church service. During one visit with her she confided that though the house was her aunt's house, the land on which the house stands belongs to another party. The family was thinking of selling the land which would essentially make her homeless.

She was understandably distressed about the possible sale. While I was in Trinidad, I contacted the owner and we met with her to discuss the situation. I provided her with my email address to contact me if they made the decision to sell. I told Euralene that if I had the money, I'd buy the land for her, thereby enabling her to live there without that additional pressure. The price for the land wasn't an astronomical amount in TT dollars but any money is too much when you don't have any to talk about. She knows that if she has occasion to travel to Canada at any time, she is more than welcome to come and stay with me and my children in my home.

I've always been a good student, I studied hard as was the expectation being raised by a teacher turned principal who was herself the epitome of high standards. Education and learning have always been a cornerstone in my life, so I guess it was inevitable that I would end up working in the field of education.

One of auntie's plans had I remained living in Trinidad was that I'd attend Bishop High School in Port of Spain, and then go on to a professional career. Auntie has always wanted the best for me, as she does for all her relatives and I believe she considers me part of her family, notwithstanding that I was married to her nephew and I'm the mother of her great niece.

Although I didn't speak until I was four years old, I started attending my great Aunt Iris' private school after she asked mom to let me go and live with her. Like auntie she was also an unmarried teacher with no children of her own and she lavished me with care and attention. Mom told me about one particular occasion

REVELATIONS

when Aunt Iris went shopping around Christmas time. She purchased so many toys and children's items at the store that the salesperson asked her, "Is that all for one child?" In her schoolteacher, proper English-speaking voice she said, "Yes it is." As was her custom she was dressed impeccably from head to toe including wearing stockings, a hat and hat pin.

I had been living with her for a while and mom had specifically asked Roy not to go to her house because it would cause problems. Unbeknownst to mom of course he went to the house anyway. As soon as I saw him, I started to cry and I wouldn't stop because, like any little child, I'd missed my father. The result was that Aunt Iris brought me back home "bag and baggage", as mom put it. My father's little stunt meant that that was the end of the privilege of living with her. Mom said that when she spoke to him about it afterwards, he just laughed. That's one hell of a sense of humour he had. He knew what was going to happen before he went and that's exactly why he did it, and he found joy in ruining that opportunity for me.

That was unfortunately not the only time that humour seemed the appropriate reaction at an inappropriate time for my father. He would come home from work at the end of the day and, as children do, I'd go running out to meet him, happy that daddy was home. Mom's often told me that I had "weak knees" as a child and Aunt Iris, God bless her, would rub my knees with brandy to help strengthen them. As home remedies go that's a doozy and an expensive one too. I would often fall down when I ran, and I have the scars on my knees as proof.

I guess I didn't have enough sense to stop running when I kept falling down. When I ran to greet dear ole dad, he would walk right past me and go into the house with a big smile on his face. He was such a wonderful father as always. Richard doesn't agree with mom though, he said, "Maybe you were clumsy." Isn't it wonderful how brothers always have a way of bringing you back down to Earth? Either way I'm just glad that I grew out of that phase, whatever you want to call it.

I was fifteen years old when Aunt Iris died, four years after we moved to Canada. I remember mom and Judy telling me that she'd intended to bequeath her house to me in her will. More than anyone else Judy was very surprised when I didn't inherit the house. Years before her death Aunt Iris had contacted mom to let her know that she had papers she wanted her to sign. We have no

REVELATIONS

way of knowing what steps she may have taken to make her desires known or if she had a will stating her intent. She'd put off sending the documents to mom and she died before she could finalize her intentions but for years "we" all knew.

After her death something odd happened during a visit to Trinidad when mom and I visited Aunt Iris' brother's home. He'd inherited her house and although I'd never met him before in my life, after our visit he inexplicably drove us to a jewelry store in town and bought me a pair of silver bracelets.

I really didn't comprehend his generosity, but I guess it was my consolation prize. I wouldn't have particularly wanted a house in Trinidad and at that age it would have been a huge responsibility to manage a property half a world away. I know people have property abroad, but it would be too much of a headache for me and it's never been something that I've wanted for myself.

A few years ago, Judy, my absolute favourite cousin in the whole wide world, died suddenly and unexpectedly long before any of us were ready to say goodbye and let her go. She was a very special woman and she's always held a special place in my heart. Richard and I used to visit her during summer breaks from school to spend time with her and our cousins in Providence, Rhode Island. Those summer breaks from school spent with her were the best. Why is there always one house that everyone seems to gravitate to and hang out at? That was Judy's house, the fun house.

It was during one of those trips that she started teaching me how to cook and another summer I started learning how to drive using her big Cadillac. Imagine learning to drive for the first time in one of those big Cadillacs from back in the day, when they were so long, they resembled a boat. Since that's the car she owned that's what I had to learn to drive. After driving a car that size it stands to reason that I feel comfortable driving any size car. Judy was a one hell of a good driver; she could drive like nobody's business and she could handle anything on wheels. Her last job before she retired was driving the transit bus in St. Petersburg, Florida.

I so wish that she was still around to see what has transpired in my life the past few years. I know she would be very proud of me as she always was of my little accomplishments. She would have loved to meet my little Key, but I know that she's watching from above

REVELATIONS

and loves her as much as we do. She was godmother to my daughter and without fail we could expect her call every April 1st, like clockwork, to relay birthday greetings and to let us know that she loved us.

I love me some Judy. Unequivocally, unending, no doubt about it and I can say that every member of my family felt the same way about her too. If they didn't, they kept it to themselves and they certainly wouldn't want to bring it up surrounded by her fans. She was, is and will always be deeply loved.

Everybody adored her; she was always full of life with a personality to match. Judy was truly a special woman in so many ways. She was caring, loving and giving to her children and her extended family. I am so very grateful to have had her in my life as long as I did. I will always cherish the memories that we shared.

Coincidentally the last occasion that I got to spend time with Judy was during a trip back home to Trinidad while she was also there on vacation, staying at her family home in San Juan. I have the pictures and memories of that trip, from her helping to secure a seat for me on a crowded, rush hour bus to our lively discussions over food at a table in the mall food court.

There was also the big family dinner that she'd helped cook one Sunday morning that we consumed and enjoyed after the church service.

One day during that trip Doreen picked us up and took us to Mount Saint Benedict, a Benedictine monastery at the top of a mountain in the Tunapuna area. It is a popular destination for religious services, pilgrimages and sightseeing. Doreen, Judy, Mom and I drove up the hairpinned, mountain road that day. As always along the way there were a lot of houses and the odd stray dog, but also a number of people making the trek on foot, on their way to and returning from the monastery.

At the last turn in the road we were greeted by the huge, multi-level, sprawling religious structure at the peak of the mountain. After exiting the car, we sat for a while under the most magnificent tree admiring the beautiful panoramic view below. It was another glorious day and it was so quiet and peaceful up there it was rarified air, you could almost feel God's presence right there with you. Judy said, "All these years I've been coming to Trinidad and this is the first time I've ever come here." That would be her last trip to Trinidad, until she flew back to take her final resting place there with her ancestors.

REVELATIONS

At one time Judy and her three sisters and their families all lived in Providence, Rhode Island. Eventually Judy and Donna moved to St. Petersburg, Florida but Maureen and Ann stayed in Rhode Island. The move to Florida made sense to me, after all the weather there was sunny and tropical just like back in Trinidad. About a year after Judy's death we were all still coming to terms with her loss when her sister Ann suddenly and inexplicably passed away.

She and Judy have been extremely close, and she'd really been having a hard time accepting that she was gone but no one saw that coming. It was an extremely painful blow for all of us, not that death is ever easy, but it was a real shock.

Death is such a final, unforgiving event. There's not usually time to say goodbye, to say sorry or to take back anything that may have been said or done. It's over, that's it and you have to hope and pray that the person knew how you felt about them and ultimately that they were loved.

About six months before Ann's death she had driven to Canada for the birth of her grandchild. One evening while she was visiting me, along with other family members who'd made the cross-border trip, I invited her to stay with us overnight. The following morning I made breakfast but Ann ate like a bird, she didn't have much of an appetite. We sat at the kitchen table talking and she told me that she likes to sit outside every morning to get some Vitamin D.

We went outside on the deck and sat on the cushioned rattan chairs to enjoy the pleasant, early morning, summer weather. As we sat there, she noticed the metal birds sitting on the deck by the family room window. Ann said, "Are those the birds?" Knowing exactly what she was talking about I said, "Yes they are." The birds were cranes that she'd had a hand in flying to me to land, as it were, on my deck.

About five years earlier mom had been in Providence for a visit. Back then she used to make the drive, or I should say she was driven over, fairly regularly. I was at home window shopping online and I happened upon a pair of beautiful cranes on sale. Unfortunately, the vendor didn't deliver to Canada but in store pick up was free of charge and I just had to have them. Since mom was already in the United States, I called Ann and asked her if she would be willing to pick the item up from the store and ship it to me. I would make the purchase

REVELATIONS

online and reimburse her for the shipping costs. She said yes without hesitation like I knew she would, she was happy to help.

That was how Ann was, just like all my family members; we're all family oriented and happy to help. The generosity doesn't extend to family only; we're all just as supportive and caring in nature to friends and loved ones.

As we sat there Ann repeated the bird escapade to me, but I've always remembered mom laughing as she'd told me what had happened, when she returned to Canada. Mom is 5 feet, 7 inches and Ann is 5 feet tall. There are two cranes the taller of which is about 3 ½ feet high and of course the box was even longer. After picking up the box at the store Ann and mom were relieved to have arrived at the post office. However, when they reached the counter the news was not good.

They were told that the box was too long to be sent by post, they would have to take it to a courier for shipping. Undaunted they found a shopping cart nearby and though the box couldn't fit very well somehow, between the two of them, they got it in the cart. Laughing along the way and getting a few curious looks from passersby, they wheeled their precious cargo to a courier location that wasn't far from the post office and shipped the box to me.

I really love those cranes and the sun has faded the paint over the years, but I bought spray paint and made them look new again. When I look at them I'm always reminded of Ann and that story. I'm glad that she got a chance to see them because it was only the brown cardboard box in which they were encased that she had seen before. I had no idea that would be the last time that we would be together. I'll always remember that beautiful, relaxing morning spent with her, just the two of us getting our Vitamin D.

I've come full circle and I realize that I have all the family that I could possibly need. I feel secure within the loving embrace of my true family, the family who have always been there for me and welcomed me without reserve or hesitation. I love you all, each and every one of you!

13 - Epilogue

One day out of the blue Richard calls me and says, "Do you remember that I was kidnapped?" The question was totally unexpected and far out of left field. I was shocked, I said, "What? When were you kidnapped?" He then disclosed his memory of a time when he was two years old and Roy had grabbed him from mom while she was out in the yard. He said he was gone for two weeks and he was taken to a house where all the faces were unfamiliar to him. As he recalls it he had no clothes on because none were taken with him. I guess Roy didn't plan ahead about taking him and getting some clothes for him to wear too.

J. P. HAMILTON

He remembers sitting on a bed naked and crying all the time because he was in a strange house with people he didn't know. He also remembers the people looking at him, almost examining him. He doesn't know if they fed him or if they even took care of him. He said it was the first time in his life that he doesn't really remember anything else. To me that's not surprising because that situation would be traumatic for anyone especially a two-year-old child. That he can remember anything from that age is unbelievable to forgetful me.

During the long conversation that touched on a number of subjects, all related to when we lived in Trinidad, my brother shared with me what he was feeling when mom left us in Trinidad. He said he felt like his world ended that day, that he was being "left to the wolf" because mom had been the buffer between him and her mother, and now he was going to be left alone with her.

At almost five years old he said that he felt abandoned, lonely, fearful, anxious, and worst of all he was always hungry during those months that he lived cross the street. It was awful hearing him say these things even though it was such a long time ago. I had no way of knowing this is what he was feeling or experiencing, I can't even recall how I felt at that time.

REVELATIONS

Auntie recently told mom that I asked her if Richard could come and live with us too. Richard and I were 4 ½ and 7 years old respectively, and there had been no sibling meeting out in the yard where we hatched a plan for me to help him come over to the other side of the road. For reasons that will remain a mystery, I decided to ask auntie if he could come and live with us. I, of course, have no recollection of the conversation or of making the request. I don't doubt the veracity of her words because there's no reason why she'd make that statement unless it was true.

I don't think that I knew or had any inkling that something was wrong but it's probably simply because I loved my brother and I missed him. Even though we didn't live that far apart it had been months of separation. Prior to that we had been together since he was born except, of course, for those two weeks when he was missing. Whatever made me ask auntie I'm just really glad that I did. I can only surmise that mom had left, my father wasn't around, and I wanted my brother to be with me. All the members of my family were gone, scattered to the winds, and I needed someone familiar around me on a daily basis.

J. P. HAMILTON

At that age I don't know where I found the courage or confidence to approach auntie with the suggestion. I'm deeply grateful to her for not only listening to that little girl but honouring her enough to follow up on her request, and providing a home to a second child. I don't believe she knew what was happening to him or how he was feeling because she would have done something about it. Whatever the reason she helped him escape the conditions in which he was living. Auntie opened the door for him to literally walk over to the other side of the street where everything may not have been perfect, how could it be with neither parent present, but there was more attention and more food to help sustain him.

After I finished speaking to Richard, I called mom to ask her about what we'd talked about. First, I asked her about what happened when she was leaving for Canada. She told us that she was leaving the day before she was scheduled to fly out. After sharing the news with us she said, "Richard looked shattered, like his world fell out below him and he went and sat down." As she's talking about it, I could hear a change in her voice as she relived the look on her young son's face, and she started to get emotional. She said, "I'll never forget the look on his face. He didn't cry, he just went and sat down and looked up at me defeated. He only said one word. Ok." What else could you say when your world has ended?

The next topic up for discussion was his kidnapping. Mom said, "Yes he was kidnapped. We were already separated at the time and one day I was sitting out in the yard with the two of you. You were five and Richard was two. I looked up and Roy was standing there looking at us. He was like that, always listening in doorways to your conversations and he would stalk you sometimes." Yes, she said the word stalk and he didn't only do it to her either.

"He came up to me and he didn't say anything. He just snatched Richard out of my arms and took off with him. I went to the police station a number of times and reported it, but they wouldn't help. They said that because he was the father, they couldn't do anything about it. After two weeks he brought him back and gave him to me."

As shocking as that may be that's not even the most shocking thing that she told me during our conversation. Mom nonchalantly said, "You know what, now that I'm talking to you about this I remember the same thing happened with you when you were two years old too."

Was two years old his magical kidnapping age or what? Like a bell goes off in his head or a little voice says, "Yo, wake up man, it's time to take her kid again and make her suffer."

As you can imagine I was none too pleased to have this little tidbit of information dropped into the puddle that was my mind. If I thought I'd turned pale before now I'm just a ghost, there would be no reflection in the mirror if I looked at it now. I said, "What are you saying?"

She continued, "When you were two years old, I told him that I was going to leave him. I was very unhappy being married to him. I was pregnant and I was always hungry, he wouldn't even give me money for food. He was so cheap with everything. One day when his mother was babysitting you at her house, I went to pick you up and she told me Roy said not to let me take you. I called your Uncle Wilfred and he went with me to the police station to report it. When I spoke to the female officer at the counter and told her his name, she said that he was her relative and then she wouldn't help me. He brought you back home after a few days."

REVELATIONS

What can you possibly say in response to your mother making such a statement? She spoke in a monotone like it was nothing; she could have been talking about the weather or what she was going to make for dinner that day. I guess the situations that she'd had to face living with my father, his behaviour and the passage of time had dulled the pain of the forced separation from her children. I know she suffered during those times, how could she not? For a mother to have to deal with something like that along with everything else would push anyone to their mental and emotional limit. How does a woman reconcile in her own mind that the man she married, the father of her child could treat her so callously?

I then asked her about the incident at the house with the knife. For our first trip back to Trinidad we were all supposed to travel together, Richard, mom and myself. Roy had unilaterally made arrangements of his own and that's how we ended up flying out by ourselves with mom arriving later during the trip. Now that I think about it, it was probably for the best that mom wasn't there when we arrived. If she had been there, she would not have put up with the whole let's take a tour of the all bus stations with my children fresh off the plane idea. Knowing her as I do now, she would not have been pleased about it, she would have made a fuss, there would have been a ruckus and it undoubtedly would not have ended well.

During the first part of the trip we stayed at my paternal grandmother's house which is located on a steep hill in Belmont. Surprisingly, Roy would visit us regularly and each time he visited he would take me into a room to talk to me privately. I don't know what he wanted to talk about, but I do know that his mother wasn't pleased about it and she brought up the subject with him more than once. He was not happy to have her input and he made his feelings on the subject very clear to her. I don't recall what he said to me during our private meetings probably because it was neither important, nor made sense and possibly because he was not being kind to my mother.

As was the plan for the rest of the trip we stayed at my cousin Judy's family home in San Juan, which was close to Aunt Edna's home at the time. One day Roy came over to the house cursing and carrying on, like the loose cannon he could sometimes be, and making disparaging remarks about mom. He was upset because we were no longer staying at his mother's house, and we basically didn't really want to have anything to do with him. This

REVELATIONS

is completely understandable because we were teenagers, he was a stranger to both of us and his behaviour since we landed in Trinidad was not appealing, to put it mildly.

In the years that we lived with Auntie Cynthia he never came to visit us once and Trinidad is a small island. He was upset that we were no longer readily accessible to him. He decided that the solution was to come over, sit outside the house with a knife, and rant about mom using expletives and threatening violence. Our protector, Walter, came to the house and chased him away. I was then sent to stay at Aunt Edna's house for a few days.

For some obscure reason Roy seemed to have had a fixation about me and I really don't understand what the fixation was about or why it existed. I don't know if he was trying to make up for lost time with all the talking that he was trying to talk to me privately, or what. And to be quite honest I really don't remember too much about it nor do I even want to remember. Nothing in association with my father has ever made any sense and it never will.

J. P. HAMILTON

Before we finished what had already been a disturbing conversation mom shared a violent incident that he tried to perpetrate against her. Like Jericho the walls had fallen down and she was getting it all off her chest. She had finally separated from him and she was living at her mother's place. Like a bad penny he showed up one day and confronted her with a cutlass in hand.

Thank God a neighbour witnessed what was about to happen, bravely stepped in to defend her and managed to wrestle the cutlass away from him. Afterwards the neighbour told him he was going to call the police and he took off like a coward. In my opinion any man who physically assaults or attempts to assault a woman is the personification of cowardice. No report was ever made to the police, so he never had to answer for any of his alleged crimes.

By this time, I can't even make reference to looking in a mirror because I have ceased to exist. Hearing her say these things was not just shocking but painful to hear them come out of her mouth. I know she didn't really want to remember or talk about any of it and I could hear the hurt in her voice as she relived it, even just in her mind. What a despicable excuse for a man he was? Who in their right mind tries to kill someone in broad

REVELATIONS

daylight in the presence of others? Not that trying to or succeeding at killing someone behind closed doors is any better, but the sheer bravado of his actions was inconceivable. There isn't anything that excuses his behaviour, nothing that she could have done that would have mitigated his actions or justified his intended level of violence.

Not once but twice her husband used her children against her as a means to extract some form of retribution. What kind of man, never mind father, does something like that not only to the mother of his child but to his own offspring? From the evidence he was a callous, immature, selfish, irrational, violent person. I was much better off for not having known him and for not having been exposed to his behaviour for longer than I was. I could have lost my mother that day, in the blink of an eye she would have been taken from us. What would have become of us then? Essentially, we would have been orphans even though one parent, who was never a parent to us, would still have been drawing breath.

I didn't ask mom but I wonder if I was a witness to my father's behaviour and violence. How much did I see as a child that I can't remember or want to remember? Was that attempt on her life just another memory that I've blocked out of my mind? How much of an impact did those traumas have on my inability or refusal to speak until I was four years old? Perhaps those incidents in my life like my brother being snatched from us for two weeks, and my separation from mom for those few days are partly to blame for why I sometimes wipe things from my mind, so I don't have to relive whatever happened.

How are you supposed to feel as a child when your parent has no interest in you? What are you supposed to think and how does that impact your self-worth? If there's anyone who ought to be interested in you shouldn't it be your parent? I believe it's more important that there were other people in your life who were not only interested in you but who also cared about you. My self-worth is important and no one else can determine my worthiness but me. I am worthy and I've always been worthy of the love and attention that every child craves and deserves but my father was not worthy of me.

I am grateful to my mother for everything she's done for me. She has not had an easy or a happy life which is the reason why I sometimes tell her, "Mom I just want you to be happy. I want you to have some happiness in your life." There have been times when I thought she should do more and be more and she certainly could've done so, if she'd chosen to because she's a very smart woman. However I can't project my expectations on her because there have been times when I've thought that I could've done more with my own life.

Her life experiences haven't always been the best, but they've definitely shaped her in more ways than any of us can ever really know. I do know that she has done the best she could for us and has always been there for us in any way that she could possibly have been. I know that whatever it was within her power to give us she gave but that she still wished she could've done more.

Let's see now, what have I learned during this unexpected journey? I have learned that my father was not only a cheapskate he was also a verbally abusive, cruel, violent, child snatcher and attempted murderer. I think that about sums it all up. There's ample, documented evidence that there are a lot of fathers in the world who are much, much worse than mine but somehow that's no comfort. I do take comfort however in the knowledge that I was lucky to have had a narrow escape from actually being raised by that him.

J. P. HAMILTON

One side of my family is a very barren, desolate place with neither emotion nor attachment. On the other side it is lush, green, fertile ground with joy and an abundance of family love in full bloom. Like the taste of a fine wine on the tip of your tongue it's rich, full bodied and very satisfying. So much so that there's not even an awareness of anything missing.

All the love, caring and attention that I've ever experienced in my life has come from the maternal side of my family. All the memories, the joy and laughter that has passed through my life are due to their love and support of mom and of us, her children, as an extension. The breadth of love that I've experienced from my family is beyond any words that I can express.

Like a lot of others, I've experienced doubts and I have insecurities even though people often compliment me and in the past have told me that I should be a model. If I had a nickel for every time someone said those words to me I would be a rich woman. After a while when you're told the same thing enough times you start believing it, whether it's something good or bad. I believed them and it was a dream for a while to accomplish that goal, to walk the catwalk with the beautiful people and wear gorgeous clothes. And I do love wearing gorgeous clothes.

When you have a dream though it isn't enough to sit back, close your eyes and expect things to happen like magic, there is some work that has to be put in. I took a couple of modelling courses and I had a portfolio created but that was the extent of my commitment to the cause. In my naivete I hoped to be discovered in a mall or grocery store or wherever, you hear stories of that happening sometimes. But modeling is a tough, unforgiving business and I am certain that my soft, vulnerable heart would not have withstood the intensity or the pressure.

A memory that stands out in my mind is at a street corner waiting for the light to change, and a little old lady beside me looks up at me and said, "Wow you have amazing legs." Another time I remember I'm walking briskly through the vegetable aisle of the grocery store and someone was coming from behind me. When the man caught up to me, he unexpectedly said, "You have great legs." I always smiled, thanked them and kept on moving at a good pace in my heels, as usual. None of those complimentary statements have ever stopped me from being down on myself, being insecure at times, thinking that I could have done much more with my life.

Eventually you come to the realization that you are where you are meant to be. You may not get there on a smooth, straight, easy path and it may take a while to get there via a circuitous route, but you will get there. You have to arrive because it's your life's path. I've come a long way since those days, I've become a lot more positive and self-assured and I know that I am exactly where I'm supposed to be.

I say my wants, goals and desires out loud. Not loud enough to raise concerns about my mental health but just loud enough for my own ears and to reinforce them in my mind. It's also important to write things down as another form of reinforcement. I write stuff down all the time, like where I want to be and what I want to do.

I make lists about everything like when I wanted to buy a house that I just loved the moment I saw it. I wrote down what I needed to buy and where I was going to put everything in the house. I put in the offer and my most magnificent real estate agent, Rosanna, advised me that someone had already put in an offer so I should be prepared for bad news. I had stepped into that house, I

REVELATIONS

had expected to get it and I've been living in it for thirteen years now. I know that if I stay positive and have a clear vision of what I want I will arrive at my destination. I believe that my dreams will come true and so many of them already have.

In the end we're all human and no matter what looks back at us in the mirror there's always something you think could be better. Things are never perfect because we all tend to judge ourselves more harshly than anyone could ever judge us. After stating your desires, you have to believe and, as they say, let go and let God do his work. Somehow it never happens as quickly as we want it to, but it will happen. Dreams that I didn't even know that I had are coming true for me and they can for you too.

I've been very fortunate in my life to have family around who have loved me and wanted the best for me. I haven't always been a positive or self-assured person because I've experienced hard times and personal hardships like everyone does but these times have fortified me and helped me to become the strong, confident person that I am today. It hasn't been easy, but it sure has been worth it. I've come a very long way and there's still a way to go because I have a lot more living to do. I am extremely proud of myself and my accomplishments, the teeny tiny ones, and the great big ones too.

The idea of keeping in touch with my children during my absence has not only snowballed into this little story it's gone way beyond that. A dam has burst and from the inevitable questions and discussions have flowed even more revelations than I could have possibly foreseen. It has promoted a level of dialogue that has never taken place before. A window into my mother's psyche has been flung open with a developing view of all that occurred before that fateful day when she jetted off to her new life in Canada.

I'm learning about the experiences that she lived through and the burdens she had to carry and conquer to keep herself afloat. Although she's opened up a lot there are still some things that are just too painful for her to discuss, think about or even put into words. She's had to overcome challenges that formed and shaped her into the person that she is today. Some of those challenges would have broken a weaker person but she has more inner strength than I ever knew she possessed.

REVELATIONS

I am very fortunate to be able to continue seeing the fulness of her development as a woman, a mother and a daughter. It makes me even prouder of her than I already am, to know what she has had to wade through and conquer to be here with us today. I feel a tremendous amount of pride knowing that I started the ball rolling and I look forward to hearing more as her story continues to unfold.

Mom has always been and continues to be the only parent that I've ever had in my life and I am very grateful for having her. Even at those times when she travels alone to Trinidad to visit her brothers, and I know that she's just a plane ride away, I still miss her a lot. She doesn't know it but somehow in my mind it always feels like she's gone, and it makes me really sad.

Thank you mom for being the best possible mother and father that you could have been to us. I am very grateful for having you as my mother and if you don't already know it, even though you have been told enough times in many ways, you mean the world to me. I love you mom!!

Manufactured by Amazon.ca
Bolton, ON